The Journey

Poems

by

Benedict Cadwallader

Cestrian Press

Front cover: The Journey, 2007 acrylic on board by Benedict Cadwallader

Cover and all illustrations by Benedict Cadwallader

First Published in 2024 by:
Cestrian Press

978-0-904448-67-2

Printed and bound in Great Britain by
Book Printing UK

These poems celebrate a life very nearly lost on
20th October 2010.
Mine.
The first ten poems were written pre-injury,
those following were written post traumatic brain injury.
After my life was saved.

ABOUT THE AUTHOR
BEFORE and AFTER

Before

Before his accident, Ben was already a prolific writer – producing plays, poetry and sketches that reflected his black humour and lateral thinking and biting wit. His work was sharp-angled and complex; that of a young man on the cusp of exploring and challenging the world in front of him.

Ben was a performer as well as a thinker; an actor and a sportsman as well as a writer. But his poetic instinct grew in strength as he journeyed through his adolescence towards adulthood. His horizons were wide and his powers of expression and poetic perception gathering apace.

These early 'Before' poems reflect his far-flung travels - Indonesia to visit family; India; Ethiopia where he worked in an orphanage and a hospice after leaving school; Hong Kong, New Zealand and Australia with friends. Ben has always been acutely observant and his poems collage aspects of the many places he visited. But the warp and weft of his creative impulse was, and remains, an exploration of love and loss.

Ben came at the world with curiosity, depth of thought and thirst for literary knowledge as well as a playfulness and a boldness laced with the uncertainty and vulnerability that comes with youth.

As a student, on his travels, with his friends, Ben loved to look at the world upside down and back to front and to explore ideas. The impulse to distil into poetry these insights into the blood, sweat and tears as well as the mystery and beauty and comedy of life, has been with him from early days. It is an impulse that has endured.

After

In the early days of Ben's recovery, he appeared disconnected from the world around him. The Ben 'before' loomed large, noisily reverberating among his family and friends. With fragmentary memories, Ben had to piece together who he was, and who he would be. Ben rediscovered himself in his creativity. He started to draw, went on to paint, and now moulds pottery. He meditates on the sounds of words. He delights in the absurd, and disconcerting people with his mischievous sense of humour. It is in his poetry, the last art form he returned to after a long period of dormancy, that he expresses himself most authentically, and connects his past and present selves.

Ben performs his poetry to friends, family, and crowded village halls. As a member of RAWD (Random Acts of Wildness Disability), Ben has started to write for the stage again and acted in the plays he has co-written. Ben the incorrigible showman has re-emerged. His decision to live, and to find out who he is now, is an act of courage. That thankfulness for life is writ large in this book.

Elaine Williams, journalist and Eléonore Berthelsen, family friends

Contents

BLANK

BLANK

AFTER

FOREWORD

By Kemal Houghton

This volume follows the re-emergence of a poet of great promise, a promise that was so nearly cut short. I first became aware of Benedict when, as part of this re-emergence, he joined the poetry groups First Thursday and Chester Poets. It was clear that there was a book to be had, but just as he'd had to relearn how to walk, he now needed someone to help him to tidy his poems. I knew who could do this. Ian Parr was an accomplished poet who understood the technicalities of verse and language better than almost anyone else.

Living in Ironbridge plus various bouts of chemotherapy meant that Ian couldn't join us for meetings, but this didn't prevent him from reading each of the poems and making often copious notes on each one. This we turned to our advantage. Benedict still had problems with his short-term memory, but Ian's notes helped to keep us on track.

Benedict had achieved much with his writing prior to the accident and so we decided that his early poems should stay pretty much in their original form. The odd word may have changed and some punctuation tweaked, but we felt that these poems should remain true to the teenager within. This then threw down the gauntlet. The new poems would have to be at least as good as the old ones. Despite the difficulties Benedict now faced, he had to re-learn the craft. Although this collection was written before his mentoring sessions with Rosanna McGlone, her input enhanced the revision process by giving Benedict an understanding of the need for constructive criticism. He was also getting out and reading his poems in public, learning again what did and did not work.

The editorial meetings then, comprised Benedict, his mother Theresia, me and Ian's notes. We read each poem along with his comments. I had been on enough panels with Ian to know where he was coming from and what sort of fixes we would need to do. Any alterations were quite properly left entirely to Benedict. Sadly Ian is not with us to see the fruition of this work but we thank him for the part he played and the encouragement he gave.

This then is a book of two halves: Benedict the emerging teenage poet and the re-emergence of the poet following a traumatic brain injury. There are two blank pages as a visual reminder of the time when he simply wasn't with us. You may see a difference between the two halves, and rightly so, as you would expect any young poet to develop their craft.

Although Benedict's journey has been a long and difficult one, his love of, and playfulness with words shines through this collection. It is a journey full of tenacity and above all else, hope. *The Journey* is not over yet and we wait with bated breath to see where he will lead us next.

June 2024

ACKNOWLEDGEMENTS

I would like to thank the late Ian Parr, my editor, who sadly died before he was able to see the finished book. He had painstakingly read and commented on each of the poems in this book and was a great help in finessing many of them. I hope this book would have made him proud. Thanks to Kemal Houghton who introduced me to Ian Parr, the Chester Poets, First Thursday poetry evenings and Wirral Poetry events. Kemal kindly stepped in for Ian Parr when he was ill, and spent many hours patiently working through Ian's notes with me. This book would not be here without Kemal's help.

To Elaine Williams and Eléonore Berthelsen, who wrote "About the author". For their endless encouragement, patience and understanding. They have known me as family friends and have greatly supported me throughout my continued recovery. To Henry Bird, who helped me choose the poems to include in this book and to arrange them in order of Before and After my injury. To Sam, Anne and Simon LeGassicke who encouraged me to have these poems published. To Mark Reeves who helped me to photograph my painting for the cover of this book and my sketches for the illustrations in this book.

To Rosanna McGlone, my first poetry course tutor, who patiently helped me to restart the process of learning about poetry writing and encouraged me to keep writing, the first formal study since my injury. To Janine Suggett, my French tutor and friend, who helped with the typography for this book. To Caroline Wilson and Duncan Morum for their proofreading.

To my family for their help with absolutely everything. To my daily support team from Brainkind. To Cheryl Bell for her advice and support. To friends, family, the medical team from Leeds General Infirmary and all who have supported and encouraged me to get this book published, thank you.

INTRODUCTION

I am Benedict Cadwallader, I am a brain injury survivor. In 2010 I suffered a life-threatening traumatic brain injury while I was studying English Literature at Leeds University, which left me with some physical and cognitive disabilities. I was unable to breathe, move, speak, read, write, or form new memories. I spent eight months in hospital, and later five years in intensive rehabilitation at TRU (Transitional Rehabilitation Unit), to relearn everything. Now I am much improved physically, but my short term memory is still impaired. With support I have been able to continue to recover.

I had been writing poetry at school and had put together and co-edited an independent creative writing magazine. I am very pleased to be writing again after quite a long pause.

The Journey is my journey in poetry through my life before and after my injury. Poems in "Before" show where I was at, at that stage in my life. The Blank pages in this book signify the period when I was "not here". Poems in "After" were written after my injury. I started writing poetry again very slowly, as the dates in this book show. It took over ten years before I started writing poetry again regularly.

In the early stages of my recovery I was not able to express myself and poetry allowed me to communicate more fully than in conversation. Writing poetry helped me to come to terms with my thoughts, feelings or ideas that I struggled with about my new situation.

This is my first individual collection of poems to be properly published! I hope I can inspire others to keep trying to improve and continue living life to the fullest. Write what you feel, write what you can, write what you know, write what you see, there is poetry in everything. I write to give thanks for my life, for my family, for my friends, for my doctors, for my surgeons, for my nurses, for my physios, for my speech therapists, for my opticians. Thank you to absolutely everyone who has helped with my recovery and for keeping me all here, changed through everything yet unchanged in heart.

BEFORE

A Lament

"He's lamenting the loss of potential memories."
Clicking, ticking, tongue against teeth.
A hand thuds into my jaw
heavy, crunching. [thunderous]
'Fucking romantic. Look around
see what you've got.'

Dark faced. Body slack, loose,
ready.
He's faster than me.
Another swing, I duck,
his knee faces my nose and
meets the back of my head.

'How did you get so pretentious?'
"That's just me" I cry
'No' He whispers
'Instinct, aggression, the same as
everyone else, nothing special'.

This is me.
Foetal. Bleeding.
He bends down,
strokes my face.

His clicking isn't anger.
Mother hen fusses now,
soothing, tutting, cleaning.
'Don't move my dear.

Poor little boy.'

He takes my hand
picks me up.
'Did I hurt you?'
I shake my head silently
'How are you now?'
"Learning".

2008

Love

I had a dream,
a dream that one day,
one day I would meet,
meet a girl who loved me,
loved me and told me,
told me she loved me.

I had a dream,
a dream that my girl,
my girl came to me,
right to me and asked me,
asked me to love her,
love her and hold her,
hold her and have
her heart.

I had a dream,
a dream that I kissed her,
kissed her and dreamed her,
dreamed her to sleep,
a deep deep pretty sleep.

I had a dream,
a dream that she slept,
slept as I opened,

opened her chest,
opened her chest and took from the nest,
took from the nest of her lungs her small heart,
her small beating heart all deep pink and blue,
as blue as the ocean as pink as a salmon.

I had a dream,
a dream that I swallowed,
swallowed her heart whole for tomorrow.
And I felt it beating,
beating inside me,
beating and beating and beating inside me.

I kept this feeling when I awoke
and now every time,
every time that I choke,
it jumps right up,
right up to my throat
and I feel it beating,
beating inside me,
beating and beating and beating inside me.

2009

Silver and Gold

A long time before tomorrow
they cut out my tongue
and call me silent sorrow,
smiling sadness, violent perception.

To scream is to drown.

They hang me heels
kicking at the clouds
amongst the sighing caress
of the willow tree.

Uncorked of a tongue
the gentle breeze shakes
my trembling heart from my mouth.
It lands softly on the wet grass
and nestles, expectant at their feet
and with it my dreams come tumbling out.

Like cotton on the wind
they rise in a mist
of silver and gold,
and their heads are filled
with cool shining streams
my golden dreams and
hopeless loss.

2009

Orpheus

4.23am and Orpheus roars,
the orange African street lamps mute
his golden mane and
nothing
can hold him.

He ripples past drunk tramps,
broken rickshaws and sleeping children
in corrugated iron huts.
And his music perforates their dreams

with a sunlight that will cool
the Abyssinian day when they wake;
a sunlight to show them every joy
and keep them quick to smile.

The earth, silent beneath his tread
becomes only more radiant;
a feature lost in harsh daylight
to all but the most faithful eyes.

4.48am and the smell of spice
granulates the warm air with curiosity.
Let us see this unknown world.
He roars again and he knows:

This time he will not look back.

2010

Before Her and I

For Helina written in Asco, Ethiopia

Last night I dreamt of our hands entwined
yours elegant and cool, smooth and tough
mine guitar calloused, small and warm
and I loved you for it.

A soft rhythm moved our hands unconscious
and our prints friction sparked a well
inside and I felt quietly fit to burst
and pour forth my soul.

But no.
My heart waltzed through your open hands
and I moved your fingernails over my lips.
The silence meant everything.

That well burst its sides and overflowed,
it outpoured a river of melancholy;
an emptiness the size and shape of your hands
lingered on mine
and I had awoke.

2010

Redemption

Written in Asco, Ethiopia

And once again he conjured the darkness
and hell opened its eyes to the world.
What a surprise -
not one man had died.

Unsatisfied its maw gaped
for want of feeding.
Salivated at the sight that was
so soon snatched from its eyes.

Oh the irony!
Man on earth weeps for his fate
not knowing what death holds:
That moment of change,
that Unconquerable love.

He clutched his blanket to himself,
laughed, then shivered.
He remembered a life of guilt,
the moment came and he was gone.

The rest is love
and hell has lost another prize.

2010

Dream

Can I hold court?
Not here it seems,
behind this throat
only laughter swells,
its ebbs and tides,
wax to wane,
fit for gurgle,
fit for burst.

My thread falters,
broken,
stack-a-toe,
and this smile unbidden
leaps to my lips
and I forget...

I forget everything,
I forget my words and my thoughts
as our lips brush
and my mirth explodes
uncontrollable, untouchable
to sing and shout,
to wish to hide and love
in this n'er forgotten
shadow world of unreal memory.

My lips played by the moonlight,
I roll inside my head,
I hurt for joy.
I will remember this dream.

2010

Raindrop

He took the steps to the
top of the hill and stood
still. Arms out, eyes shut
he screamed.

The air crowds close,
hot and heavy. Pregnant.
Each nerve strains for the
taste of warm salt rain
and the sky heaves.

It strains back at him.
A sweat begins to rise.
The contractions have begun,
he screams.

Not for himself,
for her, she who can't be silent
as her child
twists, turns, roars and rumbles
and finally
cracks free.

Each drop flings
itself down disgusted with the
free space of air surrounding it
and craving firm ground.

No time to stop and
notice each perfect sphere;
each reflected world,
as they hurtle earthwards.

All that's seen is a mass,
a blur.

He stays still,
chest heaving in the moist air,
bathing in the love a
newborn gives its mother.
He smiles.

2009

Poetry

She sits there
curled, close, cuddled, snug
in the warmth of polished
ageing wood.

Concentrating, oblivious,
smiling then serious.
I sit too. Opposite,
ignored then consulted.

The strip light glow,
not cold here but warm,
brown, grained by wood
and leather boots.

Closed, bubbled and quiet
we sit contented
alone, together
and we write.

2009

Durham Cathedral

And
an enigmatic fervour grips my breast
so I step forward all dreamlike and bereft
of the scales that of so late had held my eyes
and wept hot tears and was unsure of life.

I had not thought hard stone
could prick my mind
in cav'nous silence I found otherwise.
One word gold clad rang out unuttered
and all it said was
CUTHBERT.

2010

AFTER

Rebirth

I

My daughter's men come fast,
tearing hard and strong,
at the space between my ears.
There's nothing here can stop
this rancour,
and I leave, quite undone.

II

For where can I go?
Once all has changed
and all must be relearned,
reformed in essence,
reborn through time,
though unchanged in person.

First breath, then thought,
now speech, soon feet,
remould, reform, remember,
forget, remember, forget, remember
each turn down which life leads me
forwards into new life.

I shall not forget from
where I have come,
how far I have come,
to where I need move.

I 2015 , II 2022

Thank You

Open his throat to let him breathe,
open his stomach to let him feed,
open his head to relieve that pressure,
now gently, gently, put it all back.

So thank you surgeons,
thank you nurses,
thank you physios,
and thank you opticians.

Thank you speech therapists,
and thank you to all at the hospital,
for keeping me fed,
for keeping me hydrated

and keeping me here.
For, without you, I'd be gone,
to other plains,
and other waters,

and really, not here at all.
But I am still with you,
and though progress may be slow,
I'm back on my way.

Back on my feet,
and using my teeth,
using my voice,

to make some noise,

to make me heard,
and now I can say
that I am back.
You can't deny that!
So, just to say
Thank you.

2020

Progress

'Mother, I'm scared,
the incessant ticking of time.
On and on, never stopping.
Will it stop for me?'

*'One day son,
but not yet.
You've done that once before
yet proved it wrong.'*

'How was that mother?'
'You came back, and are still coming.'
'I have no memory of that,
yet can feel the return.
Day by day, more and more,
little by little, I can see the changes.
First I talk, then I walk, now I run.
But remembering still I struggle with.'

*'Yes son, but believe me that will come,
All else has'*

2015

Home

The cold comes home
as the sun sets
over the water,
I watch the lines drawn in the sky,
darkling silently in the knowledge of huge sound.
Where do they lead?
Only up and away,
to a place before
Home.

2016

What's Changed

What's changed you ask?
Everything.
And yet I am still me,
that hasn't.
But, I won't remember
Everything.
I've re-found my feet,
my health,
my hands,
my guitar,
my paintbrushes,
yet, I won't remember
Everything.

Time has healed much,
effort too.
But, I won't remember
Everything.
I'm looking forward,
looking back is difficult,
I want to advance,
to get on with life,
but, I won't remember
Everything.

New can be strange,
new can be difficult,
yet without new, where would we go?

We need new.
Though, I won't remember
Everything.
Keep trying and some will remain,
but, I won't remember
Everything.
Look forward, they say,
move on, they say,
yet still,
I want to remember
Everything.

2020

If it Weren't for You

If it weren't for you
at the HDU
I'd be talking to God,
not in head nor heart,
but person to person
as I did to you
once I had awoken
and found I could speak!

2014

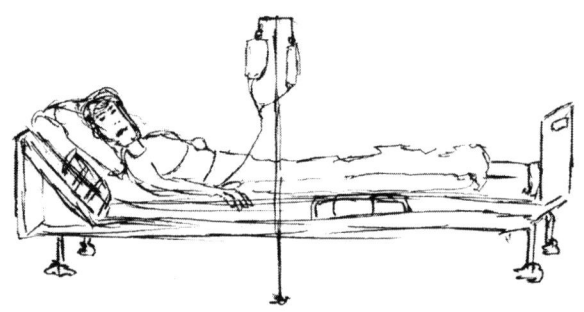

Up Too Early

Waking in the silence of the night,
the click clack non silence of the light,
hoping the pitter patter as you go
is not so loud as to wake the house.

But for the roar as you flush away,
one can only hope they're gone so deep
as not to mind nor wake so soon
before the breaking of the light.

For when morning comes you'll ask
and apologise, for making such
godawful noise. Then hope all
is forgiven for waking so soon

to find relief, before the morning
breaks.

2021

Tides

I awoke and blessed
the night
as it cradled
and hid my fear,
with fireplace aglow
pooling cold moonlight
gratefully cooling
the raw throated
chimney.
I dreamt moon;
her, with the aching
eyes and touchless
fingers. An unfelt
caress?
A cruel mistress?
I have seen her
ply
the waters and
puppet the waves,
hushing with soundless
and faceless
words
sleepless bairns
to bed, while her
long fingers
marionette the waves,
as she passively
plays.

For those souls
lost at sea,
a wry smile.
And I slept again
along with the
world.

2021

Narcissus

Stray from this path
and live the world
anew.
Feel thigh brush thigh
step by step,
murmuring to the trees'
breathy exchanges
each blade of grass
shivers and yields
to your touch.

Vanity died,
not the little death
of the French that
vanity can so often
enjoy, but the complete
cessation
of its existence.
For one.
Too short eternity

I felt.
Each.
Fragment.
Of existence that
is beauty and that
hums life like
our lungs accordion

breath.
I felt it
and it flowed
through me, and was me.

Then,
the ever vain
self reprised her
role upon the throne
that becomes only
Vanity.

2019

Change

The cheewit of the birds
waking the morning,
the sun kissed flowers
shifting silently.

Each perfect sphere of dew
resting, waiting on the leaves
for a gust of wind
to shake, and then

to fall silently to the ground.
To be absorbed by the earth,
for the cycle to begin again,
through the roots

from whence all things start,
unburdened by the constraints of time.
Growing, changing, loving, moving on,
for the world will move,

And so must I.

2021

Life

Bright light,
warm sun,
ringing green
lifts the heart
up to the horizon,
to meet the sky
and kiss the sun.

Take in the air
with each step,
and let us love,
for the world is
ours, and we must
return the love it has
shown to us, for life
is wonderful so, let us
Not
stem its flow

2021

Goodnight

Written in Devon 9.17pm

To follow the blue line
at night, is not as easy as
first it might seem.
The darkness shrouds all
but the headlight fan,
which when flanked
by towering green walls
is no fan at all.
But make it home we will,
just to home, slow and careful.
The night may have fallen
but we have not yet.
Not yet, before we have found
the comfort
of our beds!

2021

Gilgamesh

I wrote this in competition with my father and sister.

The lion sang,
Gilgamesh ran
his course, bright and
light and strong.
Fire licked his feet,
blades licked his teeth
and knifed his tongue.
Howl, roar and bid
kind rain to fall
and fall it did.
The floods rose bright,
red and
beautifully scented.

2011

Games

Must we play here
amongst these ruinous
pipes and tin cans?
Aye, we must as it is our home,
from where we have grown.

Not there on those manicured lawns,
on where the edges must not be trodden
in fear of Gran's anger
and all that might ensue.

For many a time
has joy begun here.
Here where all is not new
and old is not sacred.
With joy sprung from nothing
and nothing sprung without
Joy.

2021

Rhona

There once was a girl named Rhona
who kept falling over and over,
so her mum lead lined her shoes
so she just couldn't move.
Now she stands all day like a statue.

2021

Fred

There once was a lad named Fred
who really believed he was dead,
'til his mum told him 'wash up',
so, he had to give that up
and wash all the dishes instead.

2021

Sleepless

One long tongue fought for control
of gnashing teeth, and regretted
what was left at the end
of the bloody tasteless stump, crimson
dripped bright white,
hard shine smile, grimace,
hunger.
A man with teeth like that,
a smile like... lips...
He can eat anything he wants!

The young girl, worried at first
but comforted, warmed, cheeky.
Eat silently.
A moan.
A groan.
White in crimson.
Those teeth, that smile, those lips.
Tasteless lips, unsucked, licked,
stumped behind
that
platinum
smile.

We love you – hard, soft;
Smile my sweet,
we'll meet you again inside.
When I'm inside? Yes,

you'll be inside,
stomach churned. Don't scream, happy
enzymes savour hands, eyes, toes,
drowned, all tense and fighting,
fighting for breath.

There, there. Don't worry,
you can join all my other friends
and happy children.
What a happy tumble in my tummy!

Suck those teeth, those lips, that smile,
white glistens through
lines one or two
crimson.
Sleep happy.

2021

Fresh

The roar and
rustle as the air
breathes through the
trees,

moving softly over the
water, and tickling its
banks as I walk
around.

The lake stirs gently,
from smooth to rough
and back again
once

more, as I continue
my journey through
the crisp morning
air.

There is nothing
I can enjoy more
than the bright cool breath of this
morning.

2022

Worry

Unfulfilled and somewhat lacking,
yet to say "what" would be impossible.
Perhaps it is the feeling of
time being stolen from me.
The feeling of the potential for
happiness diminishing.
This terrifies me.

2021

The Queen

Who'd have thought
when her uncle Edward abdicated
and her father George took the throne,
that she'd become the longest lived,
longest reigning British monarch
in history.

At ninety six years old
after seventy years at the top,
one could say she'd seen
a little bit.

And don't forget about your money,
she's gazing out from
thirty three different currencies.
Whether that be your coins or your notes.
That's a famous face you can't
forget.

I salute you Elizabeth, ERII,
for all of your years with us
and all that you've done
to keep us together
on these great isles.

2022

Help Me Lord

Where shall I go?
Whom shall I meet?
Whom should I meet?
There is only one
who I wish to meet
in the end,
but not just yet
I hope.

I want to give more,
I want to be more,
I want to remember,
yet still I struggle,
only to hold on
to what has just been.

As to what could be
I can only aspire,
and work my hardest.
For without
this effort, I'd not be
here where I am,
slowly crawling
on my way back,

back to my feet,
back to the skills I'm
carefully recalling.

To take back my life
and what I once had.
To edge my way forward,
keeping that hope
that He will bring me,
as He has so far,
and kept me all here.
Working my way
back to my life.
Accepting His help
around every corner.

For, we cannot see
what will come next,
but only to trust
in Whom we must.

2021

Time

Time, time, time,
why must you move so fast
and yet so slowly?
Changing minutely
over every second,
yet only to be seen
once minutes, hours,
days, years, have passed.

All for the better?
I can only hope
and strive for more,
so as to bring everything up,
bring everything together
and hold it all down.
To come back from nothing,
and yet still be improving!

Living for more and more.
Each day after day,
each year after year.
I won't notice the changes
yet still they come,
silently remoulding
All that I know
and All that I am.

All I can be
is only thankful.
Hunkering down,
reshaping all that
once was and all that could be
is no silent feat,
though silent it may be.
Yet, shout it I must.

As I come back
to the world I so nearly left.

2021

Where We Must

Behind these thoughts
only darkness swells.
Flickering silently
like the shadows cast by
a dancing flame.

Help me please,
before all is engulfed.
Swallowed by the
passing of time.

Let not this passage of life
come to no more,
for I do wish to arrive,
to come into something

more than
what can be foretold.
Something bold
with which

I can grasp my future,
as I move forward
into the unknown
so as to become known.

To hold firm ground
yet not stand still,
for onwards is where
I must be going.

2021

New Year's Eve 2021/22

Morning has not yet broken,
we must wait quite a bit for that,
yet, look at those lights!
Those joyous explosions in the
sky.

Those that mark the midnight,
with the hope and expectation
of a new start.
What will come?

We can only hope for
something more,
for something better,
after a year that's been lost.

But, just keep on going,
keep on going we must,
as we have learned so much
and all is not lost.

We must keep moving on,
into the unknown,
for, who can predict
what will come next?

2021/22

Shelter

Our eyes play as a window through life,
opened at birth to take in all the
wonders of this world.
Watch us grow,
watch us change.

Watch this garden of time
move us onwards
to take the next step
along this path, down which
life will move us.

Break forth into the fields
and run through the maze
to that singular tree that
presides over all beneath
its branches.

2022

The Will To Move

Shaping one's time
as on a potter's wheel,
for with every turn a new
cycle begins and another ends.

Although without finality
as this wheel will continue to spin,
shaping our worlds
and moving us forward.

With each new turn,
how we work and how we move
will always change
what we are.

Although at our heart
is that one constant,
the being of being.
That shall not move,

although time may change
how we do.
Where can we find this turn?
Only from within.

Before all else,
before anything else,
this one concern
will remain the constant:

It is necessary to
Progress.

2022

My Way Back

Crushed but whole,
can I come back?
Back from this ruinous
untorn crumpling?
Yes I can,
and I must,
for I am still here,
although somewhat changed.

Altered by the passing
of time and experience,
yet as I return
I will not forget
from where I have come.
As I must aim for more
and hold on
to what is to come.

As things will change,
but I must,
and will find
My way back.

2022

Moving on

Come to the edge
and look down to the water
that laps quietly.
Notice the rhythm,
the soft lap, pause, lap, pause,
as back and forth
the tide hurries unhurriedly in and out,
eternally.

Life will move as such.
However fast it feels,
however slow it feels,
things will come and go
and come again.
We can only move with time,
as things do change, and we must with them.

We must just make what we can,
form and reform,
before all is gone and we can no longer.

2022

Gekko

Bask on the warm tiled floor.
No care in the world but for to
enjoy the sun and the rich green
of the foliage that surrounds all.

Taste the air around
and savour the moist warmth
of everything, now let us catch that,
zzzt, zzzt, snap.

Mmm, hunger sated,
for now let us
rest again

2022

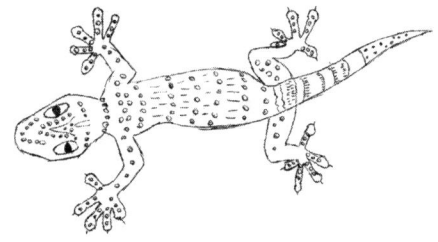

I

Homing

May I find my way?
This wandering life,
in which I can only
wander, hoping to move on,
move on to new,

move on to better?
But only to move.

How many more times?
How many more times,
must I start, only to
find myself lost?

Lost within everywhere,
lost within nowhere,
but lost nonetheless.

I can only wish to come
to somewhere new,
to somewhere calm,
and somewhere
Home.

2021

II

Hold Fast

Moving round and turning
upwards,
shall I find the light?
Help me move on,
help me move up,
help me reach more.
Where should I go?

Let me find my way,
to something more,
to something new,
and something kind.

Let me see the light.
Let me have more light.
Open up to the world
and spread my branches,
spread my roots.
Let me stand firm,
let me stand fast,
and let me stand
Forever.

2021

III

Me

Thirty years on this Earth,
when I very nearly only had nineteen,
who'd have thought I could remain
so long, when life had so nearly slipped away.

But, keep on looking on,
looking forward I must.
As things will keep on improving,
little by little, mite by
mite.

Each day unseen
something more will come.
Unnoticed at first but as I live on,
these changes ring out much
louder

and stronger
as my life
continues.
I will try to improve
in all that I
can.

In all that I must and will

to move into a life
I can live to the fullest,
enjoying my time, as it continues
to surprise us
all!

2022